Extreme
SNOWMOBILING

Blaine Wiseman

Weigl Publishers Inc.

Published by Weigl Publishers Inc.
350 5th Avenue, Suite 3304, PMB 6G
New York, NY 10118-0069

Website: www.weigl.com

All of the Internet URLs given in the book were valid at the time of publication. However, due to the dynamic nature of the Internet, some addresses may have changed, or sites may have ceased to exist since publication. While the author and publisher regret any inconvenience this may cause readers, no responsibility for any such changes can be accepted by either the author or the publisher.

Library of Congress Cataloging-in-Publication Data available upon request.
Fax 1-866-44-WEIGL for the attention of the Publishing Records department.

ISBN 978-1-60596-134-7 (hard cover)
ISBN 978-1-60596-135-4 (soft cover)

Printed in China
1 2 3 4 5 6 7 8 9 0 13 12 11 10 09

Weigl would like to acknowledge Getty Images as one of its primary photo suppliers for this title.

Every reasonable effort has been made to trace ownership and to obtain permission to reprint copyright material. The publishers would be pleased to have any errors or omissions brought to their attention so that they may be corrected in subsequent printings.

EDITOR: Heather C. Hudak
DESIGN: Terry Paulhus
LAYOUT: Kathryn Livingstone

EXTREME SNOWMOBILING

CONTENTS

WHAT ARE THE X GAMES?

The X Games are an annual sports tournament that showcases the best athletes in the extreme sports world. Extreme sports are performed at high speeds. They are often dangerous for the participants. The X Games celebrate the skill, dedication, and determination of the athletes, as well as the challenge and difficulty of the sports.

The X Games began as the Extreme Games in 1995. The following year, the name was shortened to X Games. In 1995 and 1996, the games were held in the summer. They featured a wide variety of sports. These included skateboarding, inline skating, BMX, street luge, sky surfing, and rock climbing.

The popularity of the X Games made it possible for more sports to be showcased. In 1997, the Winter X Games began. The Winter X Games feature sports such as snowboarding, skiing, and snowmobiling. Today, there are Summer and Winter X Games each year.

Some of the best snowmobilers in the world compete in the X Games. These snowmobilers perform extreme moves and race at high speeds, in front of large crowds, on some of the best mountains in the world.

TECHNOLINK

Learn more about the X Games at **expn.go.com**.

X FEST

The X Games are about more than sports. Each year, musical acts from all over the world perform for fans at the X Games. X Fest is the name for the musical portion of the X Games. It features some of the best-known punk rock, hip hop, and alternative music artists of the time. These artists perform between sporting events and keep the crowds entertained and excited for the competitions.

WHAT IS SNOWMOBILING?

Snowmobiling is a sport that requires skill, strength, and courage. Snowmobilers race across the snow on a fast, heavy machine called a snowmobile. Snowmobiles can travel at speeds faster than 100 miles (160 kilometers) per hour. A track or tread at the back of the snowmobile pushes the vehicle to move, and a pair of skis at the front steer through the snow. To turn, the snowmobiler shifts the handlebars and leans from side to side, just like riding a bike.

Snowmobiles are used as the main mode of transportation in some parts of the world. It may be faster to use a snowmobile than a car in snowy or icy places. However, in most places, snowmobiles are used only for **recreation**.

Timeline

1908 – The Lombard Log Hauler is built. This is the first machine designed for snow travel.

1913 – Virgil White builds the first "snowmobile."

1922 – Fifteen-year-old J. Armand Bombardier designs his first snowmobile.

1927 – Carl Eliason receives the first **patent** for a snowmobile.

1954 – David Johnson, of Polaris Industries, designs and builds the first recreational snowmobile.

Snowmobiles do not have a long history. However, they have gone through many changes in the past century. In 1908, the first machine was built for traveling in the snow. This machine, called a "log hauler," was designed for hauling logs through the snow.

The word "snowmobile" was first used by Virgil White, of New Hampshire. In 1913, White converted his Model T Ford automobile to drive on snow, using a track and ski system, much like today's snowmobiles.

Snowmobiles resemble motorcycles built for snow.

In 1922, Joseph-Armand Bombardier of Quebec, Canada, designed his first snowmobile. Bombardier was only 15 years old at the time. Fifteen years later, he started his own company and began selling snowmobiles. Today, his company still builds snowmobiles, as well as other vehicles, including trains and airplanes.

Another leader in snowmobile manufacturing is Polaris. This company began as a farm equipment builder. Polaris developed its first snowmobile in 1954. This was the beginning of recreational snow machines. By 1957, Polaris had stopped making farm equipment to focus on snowmobiles.

1957 – Polaris begins shifting its focus from farm equipment to snowmobiles.

1968 – Ralph Plaisted uses snowmobiles to lead an expedition to the North Pole.

1970s – Hundreds of companies begin making snowmobiles.

1998 – Snowmobiling is added to the Winter X Games.

ALL THE RIGHT EQUIPMENT

There are many different types of snowmobiles. Some are designed for racing, while others are made for performing jumps and tricks. It is important to choose the right sled. Every rider is different, and using the wrong sled can be dangerous.

Snowmobiling is a winter sport, so protection from cold weather is needed. A warm jacket, pants, gloves, socks, and boots will keep the snowmobiler warm. Dressing in layers is a good winter safety technique. Each layer should be suited to different weather conditions. If the temperature warms up or the rider becomes warm from being active, layers can be removed so that the snowmobiler does not get too warm. If it cools, layers can be added again to keep warm.

Safety equipment is an important part of snowmobiling. Snowmobilers should be well protected from crashes, rollovers, and other possible accidents.

ACCESSORIZE IT!

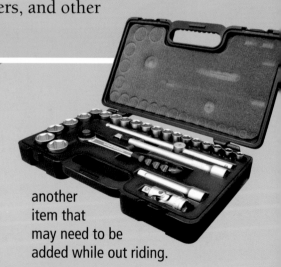

Snowmobiles are **mechanical** machines, so they can break down. It is important to know how to fix problems when they occur. It is a good idea to carry a tool kit. Tool kits should have basic tools, such as screwdrivers and wrenches, as well as some parts, such as spark plugs and drive belts. Oil is another item that may need to be added while out riding.

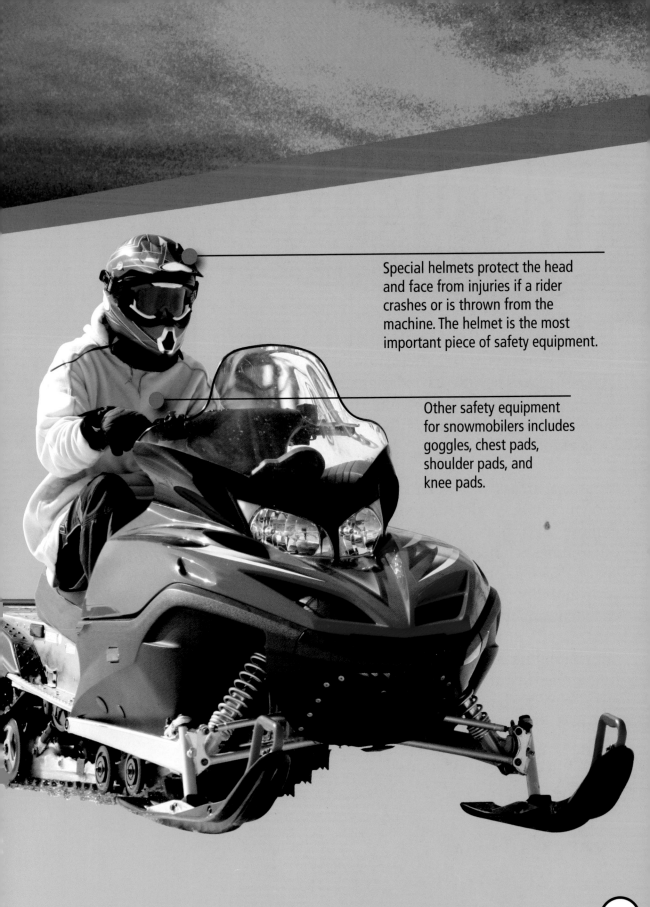

Special helmets protect the head and face from injuries if a rider crashes or is thrown from the machine. The helmet is the most important piece of safety equipment.

Other safety equipment for snowmobilers includes goggles, chest pads, shoulder pads, and knee pads.

SURVEYING THE VENUE

People often head to nearby parks and resorts to ride their snowmobiles. These places usually have designated trails for snowmobiles. Signs list trail rules and speed limits, making the activity both safe and fun for everyone.

Mountain areas can be an ideal venue for snowmobiling. With long trails, open spaces to explore, steep hills, and natural obstacles, mountains offer endless choices for all skill levels. Wide open spaces, such as prairies, also are great places for snowmobiling. Large fields and rolling hills offer excellent opportunities for all types of snowmobiling.

Snowmobiling competitions, such as the X Games, use humanmade courses that feature a combination of flat areas, curves, sharp turns, and different sizes of jumps. The best snowmobilers in the world can ride on all types of terrain at high speeds, and can perform many different types of **aerial** stunts.

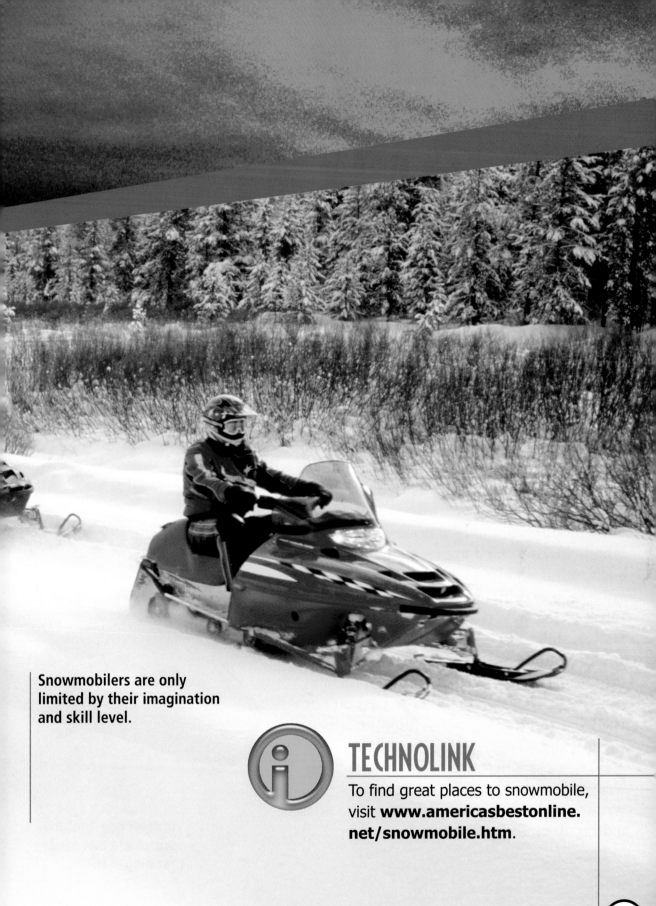

Snowmobilers are only
limited by their imagination
and skill level.

TECHNOLINK

To find great places to snowmobile,
visit **www.americasbestonline.
net/snowmobile.htm**.

SNOWMOBILE FREESTYLE

Snowmobile Freestyle was added to the Winter X Games in 2007. The event features 10 snowmobilers. Each takes turns racing through a course that has jumps ranging in height from 60 feet (14 meters) to 100 feet (30 m). After each round, the top riders move on to the next round, with one snowmobiler leaving as the gold medal winner. This event tests the riders' skill, style, and creativity.

Snowmobilers are judged on several factors, which are combined to give them a score for each round. Judges look for execution, volume, and difficulty. Execution refers to the style that the snowmobiler has while doing the tricks. Volume means how high and far the snowmobile travels through the air during the tricks. Difficulty is based on both the trick and the landing. Difficult tricks include moves such as flips and twists, as well as tricks where the rider lets go of the sled in the air. Landing with no hands, or without holding the handlebars, is considered a difficult landing.

In Freestyle, better scores are awarded for bigger tricks.

Chris Burandt won gold in Freestyle at the 2007 X Games.

PAST WINNERS

2009
Gold: Joe Parsons
Silver: Justin Hoyer
Bronze: Heath Frisby

2008
Gold: Levi LaVallee
Silver: Joe Parsons
Bronze: Heath Frisby

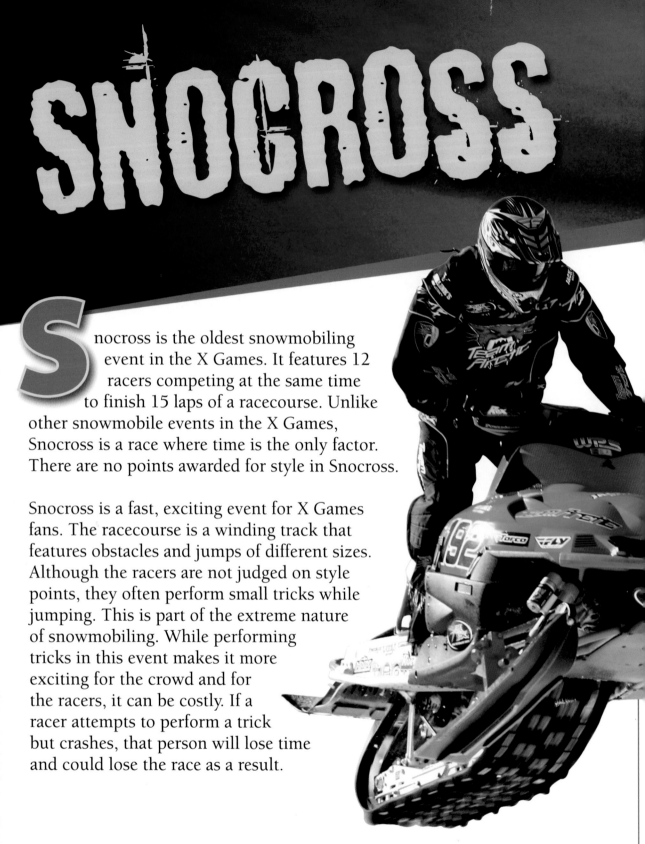

SNOCROSS

Snocross is the oldest snowmobiling event in the X Games. It features 12 racers competing at the same time to finish 15 laps of a racecourse. Unlike other snowmobile events in the X Games, Snocross is a race where time is the only factor. There are no points awarded for style in Snocross.

Snocross is a fast, exciting event for X Games fans. The racecourse is a winding track that features obstacles and jumps of different sizes. Although the racers are not judged on style points, they often perform small tricks while jumping. This is part of the extreme nature of snowmobiling. While performing tricks in this event makes it more exciting for the crowd and for the racers, it can be costly. If a racer attempts to perform a trick but crashes, that person will lose time and could lose the race as a result.

Jeff Snow has been in several X Games Snocross competitions.

Snocross competitions take place on Buttermilk Mountain in Colorado.

PAST WINNERS

2009
Gold: Tucker Hibbert
Silver: Robbie Malinoski
Bronze: Dan Ebert

2008
Gold: Tucker Hibbert
Silver: Brett Turcotte
Bronze: D.J. Eckstrom

SPEED & STYLE

Speed & Style was added to Winter X Games 12 in 2008. Eight riders compete in Speed & Style. This event combines elements of the Freestyle and Snocross events, including a race and tricks. Participants must complete the racecourse while also performing tricks. The tricks are judged, and these points are combined with the race time to determine a winner.

Cory Davis won third place in Speed & Style at X Games 13.

In a Speed & Style event, each race features two riders at one time. The winner of each race moves on to the next round until only the champion is left. The course has two tracks, one for each racer. When the first lap is complete, the riders switch tracks. This way, each rider will have a turn on both tracks. Half of the participants' score comes from their time, and the other half is judged in the same way as the Freestyle event.

People can watch the Speed & Style competition take place in person.

PAST WINNERS

2009
Gold: Joe Parsons
Silver: Levi LaVallee
Bronze: Cory Davis

2008
Gold: Levi LaVallee
Silver: Sam Rogers
Bronze: Joe Parsons

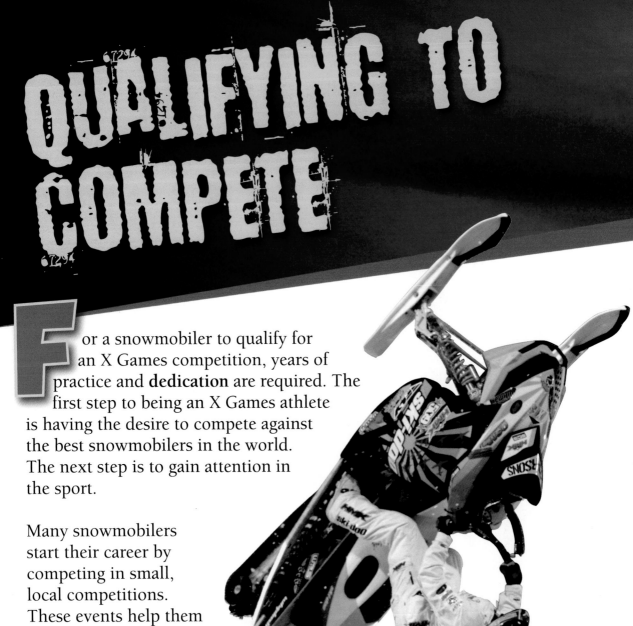

QUALIFYING TO COMPETE

For a snowmobiler to qualify for an X Games competition, years of practice and **dedication** are required. The first step to being an X Games athlete is having the desire to compete against the best snowmobilers in the world. The next step is to gain attention in the sport.

Many snowmobilers start their career by competing in small, local competitions. These events help them adjust to the challenges that competitions offer, such as **pressure** and excitement.

Professional snowmobilers practice often in order to be able to perform extreme tricks on their machines.

TECHNOLINK

To learn more about qualifying, go to **ehow.com/how_2062102_qualify-winter-x-snowmobiling-events.html**.

These events are a great place to meet other snowmobilers who may be trying to qualify for the X Games. Talking to like-minded athletes will help riders learn new ways to perform tricks and compete.

In many places where snowmobiling is popular, riders can join teams, leagues, clubs, and associations. These are groups of snowmobilers who come together to compete against each other or to practice together. Joining one of these groups is a great way to practice, talk to other snowmobilers, and gain exposure to potential sponsors.

The final step to qualifying for the X Games is to earn a spot by performing well at certain competitions. The judges who choose X Games participants attend other competitions and **scout** world-class snowmobilers. Snowmobile clubs, leagues, teams, and associations, as well as **sponsors**, are a great way to find out where and when X Games judges will be scouting.

Only the top snowmobile riders qualify to compete in the X Games.

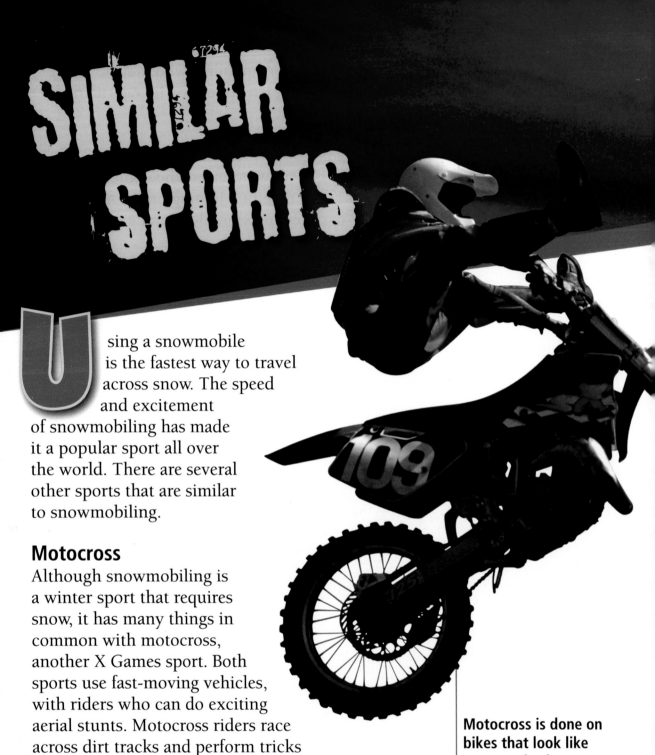

SIMILAR SPORTS

Using a snowmobile is the fastest way to travel across snow. The speed and excitement of snowmobiling has made it a popular sport all over the world. There are several other sports that are similar to snowmobiling.

Motocross

Although snowmobiling is a winter sport that requires snow, it has many things in common with motocross, another X Games sport. Both sports use fast-moving vehicles, with riders who can do exciting aerial stunts. Motocross riders race across dirt tracks and perform tricks on jumps and obstacles.

Motocross is a popular sport in many places around the world, especially in California and Arizona in the United States, as well as parts of Australia and Canada.

Motocross is done on bikes that look like motorcycles but are specially designed for rough terrain and racing.

Dogsledding

The dogsled can be considered the original snowmobile. A team of dogs pulls a sled, while the driver steers it. People have been traveling by dogsled for thousands of years. In the Far North, this is sometimes the only way to travel. Dogsledding has become a sport in many areas of the North. Popular places for dogsledding are Minnesota and Alaska in the United States, as well as parts of Canada, Sweden, and Russia.

Bobsledding

Bobsledding is another winter sport that uses a sled as a vehicle. The bobsled, however, does not have a motor or a team of dogs. Teams are made up of two or four people who sit together in the sled and slide down a track made of ice. The sled can reach speeds of 85 miles (140 km) per hour while the team steers it through the course.

Jet Skiing

A summer sport that is similar to snowmobiling is jet skiing. Jet skis look like snowmobiles, but they are built for driving across water. People use jet skis on lakes and rivers all over the world. Waves can be used as jumps and obstacles for a jet ski. Jet skiing is popular all over the United States, as well as in Holland, Mexico, and Canada.

UNFORGETTABLE MOMENTS

Throughout the history of the X Games, there have been many unforgettable moments. Snowmobiling events have seen riders pushing the limits by attempting new tricks and **maneuvers**, leaving lasting memories for fans and other riders.

In 2009, Winter X Games 13 saw the introduction of a new event. The Next Trick competition was a great success for both the riders and the fans. Next Trick features snowmobilers attempting to complete one trick each. The riders fly through the air after launching off a large jump. Each rider tries to outdo the others by landing a bigger, better trick.

Dane Ferguson was one of four competitors in the first Next Trick event.

Despite his Next Trick loss, Levi LaVallee has won other X Games medals.

Fans watching the competition on TV all over the United States were invited to text in their favorite, helping to choose a winner. However, three of the four riders did not complete their tricks. As a result, Dane Ferguson of Alaska won the event. Ferguson's trick was his own invention, called a "Twist Off." The trick is a flip, combined with a twist.

During the same competition, Levi LaVallee, who had already won a silver medal in the Speed & Style event, promised to amaze everyone by attempting a trick that no snowmobiler had ever done. Lavallee soared off the jump, and as he flew through the air, completed two backflips. However, he landed hard and was thrown off his sled when he hit the ground. This meant that LaVallee did not complete the trick.

Although he did not land the trick, the crowd cheered wildly, and LaVallee celebrated with friends and other riders. He had attempted the first double backflip in any snowmobile competition. After the event, LaVallee said that he was happy to ride away without injury and planned to keep practicing the trick for future events.

AROUND THE WORLD

Newberry, Michigan

Newberry is surrounded by beautiful natural areas, which are covered in snow during the winter. There are 210 miles (338 km) of groomed trails leading out of Newberry, which join with trails from other surrounding areas. North of Newberry, snowmobilers are treated to the beautiful Tahquamenon Falls, which freeze during the winter, creating beautiful, natural ice sculptures.

ATLANTIC OCEAN

West Yellowstone, Montana

With 580 miles (933 km) of groomed trails, West Yellowstone is considered the best place to snowmobile in America. The trails begin in town, and snowmobiles even share the roads with cars. Leaving town, sledders can explore 180 miles (290 km) of trails inside Yellowstone National Park and 400 miles (644 km) outside of the park.

PACIFIC OCEAN

Revelstoke, Canada

One of the best-known snowmobiling areas in all of Canada is Revelstoke, British Columbia. Located in the Rocky Mountains, the area around Revelstoke has giant mountain peaks and deep powder. Groomed trails provide a safe environment for all skill levels.

1. Aspen, Colorado

ARCTIC OCEAN

ARCTIC OCEAN

Kuusamo, Finland

Kuusamo is located in Finnish Lapland, in the Far North of the country. There are 310 miles (500 km) of trails in the area, which cover snow-swept plains, lakes, and beautiful wilderness areas. Finland offers some of the best snowmobiling in Europe.

Bjorkliden, Sweden

In the northwestern region of Swedish Lapland, snowmobilers can find some of Europe's most beautiful mountains. Crossing the snow-covered mountains and frozen lakes, snowmobilers can explore hundreds of miles of trails. Lucky sledders might catch a glimpse of the Northern Lights or a herd of reindeer.

PACIFIC OCEAN

INDIAN OCEAN

Lake Baikal, Russia

Lake Baikal is the world's deepest lake. Found in the Russian region of Siberia, the area receives large amounts of snow and is cold for much of the year. Leaving from the town of Listvyanka, snowmobilers can explore the crystal clear ice of Lake Baikal and the surrounding Siberian **tundra**.

CURRENT STARS

LEVI LAVALLEE

HOMETOWN
Longville, Minnesota

BORN
August 31, 1982

NOTES
Nickname is Launchin' Levi LaVallee because of his aerial stunts

Attempted the first-ever double backflip in competition at Winter X Games 13

Won gold medals in Freestyle and Speed & Style at Winter X Games 12

TUCKER HIBBERT

HOMETOWN
Driggs, Idaho

BORN
June 24, 1984

NOTES
Tucker's father, Kirk Hibbert, became the oldest competitor in X Games history when he participated in the Snocross event at Winter X Games 4. He was 42 years old.

Is a professional motocross racer

Was the youngest X Games gold medallist, at age 15, and has won a total of nine X Games medals

T.J. GULLA

HOMETOWN
South Hero, Vermont

BORN
March 20, 1981

NOTES
Began racing at seven years old

Says his biggest influence is his father

Has won three X Games medals—one gold and two bronze

DANE FERGUSON

HOMETOWN
Anchorage, Alaska

NOTES
Began using a snowmobile in 2000 for transportation into the mountains so he could snowboard

Concentrated on playing hockey for 18 years before switching to snowboarding and snowmobiling

Did not like snowmobiling at first and would have other people drive him to the top of hills so he could snowboard down

LEGENDS

BLAIR MORGAN

HOMETOWN
Prince Albert,
Saskatchewan, Canada

BORN
October 9, 1975

NOTES
Has won five X Games
Snocross gold medals

Is considered the greatest Snocross
snowmobiler in history

Nicknamed
Superman

RALPH PLAISTED

HOMETOWN
Wyoming, Minnesota

BORN
September 30, 1927

NOTES
Became the first person to
reach the North Pole by
snowmobile, in 1968

Served in the Navy in
World War II

Ralph and his family
once lived in the
wilderness of
Saskatchewan,
Canada for 15 months.
They survived by
growing and catching
their food.

Died on September
8, 2008

JOSEPH ARMAND BOMBARDIER

HOMETOWN
Valcourt, Quebec, Canada

BORN
April 16, 1907

NOTES
Built his first snowmobile at age 15

Made vehicles for mining, forestry, and oil industries, as well as for the military

Sold the first Ski-Doo—a brand of snowmobile—in 1959

DAVID JOHNSON

HOMETOWN
Roseau, Minnesota

NOTES
Built the first Polaris snowmobile

While serving in World War II, he sent some of his earnings to his friends Edgar and Allan Hetteen to start their company "Hetteen Derrick & Hoist," which later became Polaris Industries

Sold his first machine and built a second so he could tow the first when it needed to be fixed

THE 10 QUESTION QUIZ

1 In what year were the first Winter X Games held?

2 Who first used the term "snowmobile"?

3 What piece of equipment protects the head and face from injury?

4 How many snowmobilers take part in the Freestyle event?

5 What sport is similar to snowmobiling, but uses water instead of snow?

6 What snowmobiling event was added to the Winter X Games in 2009?

7 Who attempted the first double backflip at the Winter X Games?

8 Where are the Winter X Games held?

9 What area of northern Sweden and Finland is excellent for snowmobiling?

10 Who was the first person to reach the North Pole by snowmobile?

Answers: 1. 1997 2. Virgil White 3. A helmet 4. 10 5. Jet skiing 6. Next Trick 7. Levi LaVallee 8. Aspen, Colorado 9. Lapland 10. Ralph Plaisted

RESEARCH

www.kidzworld.com/article/3905-snowmobiling-101

www.amsnow.com/sno/default.aspx

www.snowtracks.com/us.htm

www.ussaprostar.net

Many books and websites provide information on snowmobiling. To learn more, borrow books from a library, or surf the Internet.

Most libraries have computers that connect to a database for researching information. If you type in a keyword, you will be connected with a list of books in the library that have information on that topic. Non-fiction books are arranged numerically, using their call number. Fiction books are arranged alphabetically by the author's last name.

GLOSSARY INDEX

aerial: taking place in the air

dedication: commit time to a task

maneuvers: movements that require skill and care to perform

mechanical: working or made by machines

patent: government grant giving a person the right to sell, make, or use an invention

pressure: influence to make someone do something

recreation: activity that is done for fun

scout: to look for people with special talent to become part of a team or organization

sponsors: people or companies that fund certain activities

tundra: vast, treeless land in northern regions where the ground remains permanently frozen